The Two Good Brothers

A folk tale from Korea
retold by Lindy Kelly
illustrated by Donna McKenna

There were once two brothers who were also good friends. When they grew up, the older brother married and moved away from home and the younger one stayed at home with their mother. Both brothers worked on the family farm, planting and harvesting their rice crops.

One day, after a very good harvest, the brothers were bagging their rice. They put the rice into sacks and divided the sacks into two equal piles.

"I'd like you to have an extra sack," said the older brother, "because you take care of our mother."

"No," said the younger brother. "You should have an extra sack because you have a family to feed."

The two brothers tried to persuade each other to take one more sack of rice, but neither would agree. So each brother took home the same number of sacks.

That night, the older brother decided he would sneak over to his brother's house and add an extra sack to his brother's rice. So he took one of his sacks and crept through the darkness to his younger brother's place. He left the sack with the rest of his brother's rice, and then he ran home, feeling good about what he'd done.

The next morning, the older brother counted his sacks of rice. He had the same number of sacks that he'd had *before* he'd visited his younger brother!

"What's going on?" he thought.
That night, he crept over to his brother's house again with a sack of rice. The next morning, he counted his sacks, and still he had the same number.

"I don't understand what's happening," he said to his wife. "I've taken two sacks of rice around to my brother's house, but I still have the same number of sacks as I had in the beginning!"

"Maybe you didn't count your sacks properly," said his wife. She counted them herself and gave one to her husband. "Take this to your brother's house tonight," she said. "Then I'll count the sacks again tomorrow morning."

That night, her husband crept through the darkness toward his younger brother's house, carrying the rice. The moon was behind a cloud, and it was dark.

Crash! The older brother bumped into something and fell to the ground, clutching the rice to his chest. "What was that?" he cried out. At the same time, he heard another voice saying "What was that?" in the darkness.

Just then, the moon came out from behind the cloud. The older brother peered into the gloom. On the ground in front of him, he could see his younger brother holding a sack of rice. The two brothers looked at each other in surprise.

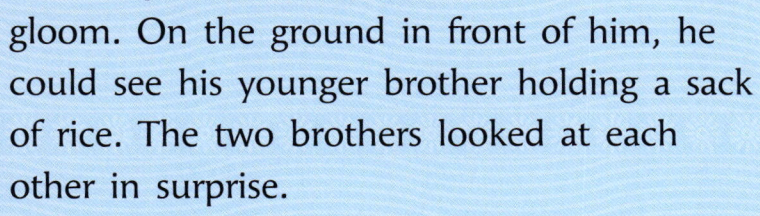

"I was bringing you an extra sack of rice," the younger brother said. "I think you need it more than me because you have a family to feed. I've crept through the darkness for the past two nights and left a sack at your house, but in the morning, I still have the same number of sacks!"

The two brothers looked at each other and then at their sacks of rice. They sat in the moonlight and laughed and laughed.